The Great Houdini

DARING ESCAPE ARTIST

The Great Houdini

MASTER ESCAPE ARTIST

by Louis Sabin

illustrated by Allan Eitzen

Troll Associates

Library of Congress Cataloging-in-Publication Data

Sabin, Louis.
   The Great Houdini, daring escape artist / by Louis Sabin;
illustrated by Allan Eitzen.
     p.   cm.
   Summary: Follows the life and exploits of the renowned magician
and escape artist.
   ISBN 0-8167-1769-9 (lib. bdg.)   ISBN 0-8167-1770-2 (pbk.)
   1. Houdini, Harry, 1874-1926—Juvenile literature. 2. Magicians—
United States—Biography—Juvenile literature. [1. Houdini,
Harry, 1874-1926. 2. Magicians.] I. Eitzen, Allan, ill.
II. Title.
GV1545.H8S23 1990
793.8'092—dc20
[B]
[92]   89-5170

The Great Houdini

DARING ESCAPE ARTIST

"Ladies and gentlemen! Silence, please!"

The boys and girls stopped talking. They watched the circus ringmaster, a nine-year-old boy grandly waving his father's top hat. The circus was taking place on a vacant lot in Milwaukee, Wisconsin. There were rides in a cart pulled by a large dog. There were games, joke tellers, and a juggler.

"And now," the ringmaster went on, "you are about to see the most daring, unusual act ever performed anywhere. It is my pleasure and privilege to bring you Ehrich Weiss, the Prince of the Air!"

The children applauded wildly as a thin, brown-eyed boy stepped forward. He was wearing knee-length pants, called knickers, just like those worn by the other boys. But Ehrich wanted to look like a real circus performer. So he had added a pair of bright red stockings. That was his complete costume. He had left his shirt and shoes behind a tree.

Ehrich climbed a wooden ladder that was leaning against a tree. Moving like a monkey, he scampered along a stout branch to his trapeze. The trapeze was made of two ropes holding a cut-off broomstick. But to Ehrich it was a fine piece of equipment for his very first performance as an acrobat.

The dark-haired youngster swung from the bar, switching hands on the stick as he flew through the air. Then, suddenly, he changed direction and for a moment sat on the bar. Next, he flipped backwards and down and around. Holding onto the bar with one knee and dangling upside down, Ehrich stretched his arms wide and grinned.

"How about that, folks?" the ringmaster cried out.

The audience applauded and cheered. Ehrich was a terrific acrobat. And as they clapped, he did three more flips and jumped lightly to the ground.

"That's not all, folks!" the ringmaster said. "Wait till you see this! First, I need two volunteers. Don't be shy. Step right up!"

A boy and a girl came forward. The ringmaster stood them next to Ehrich, who was holding up a long piece of rope.

"I will put my hands behind my back," Ehrich said. "One volunteer will tie my hands as tightly as possible. The other volunteer will watch and make sure there is no cheating."

Ehrich's hands were tied firmly. The children were sure he would never be able to undo all those knots. But Ehrich didn't look at all worried. He smiled at everyone and began counting. "One . . . two . . . three . . . presto!" He spread his arms wide and threw the rope to the ringmaster.

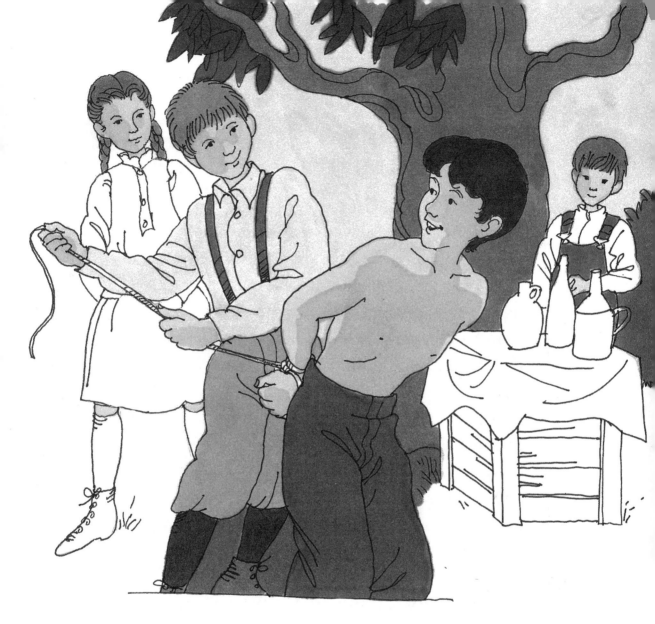

"Wow!"

"Wonderful!"

"How'd you do it?"

Ehrich smiled. "It's magic," he said.

Ehrich Weiss enjoyed magic as much as the audiences he performed for. These thrills would only increase when Ehrich later took the stage name of Harry Houdini. As Houdini, he would soon be recognized the world over as one of the finest magicians of all time. His fame would grow with every dazzling trick he performed. Even the name "Houdini" would eventually come to mean someone doing impossible, incredible escapes and baffling magic tricks.

One of the finest magicians of all time—such an idea never occurred to Cecilia and Samuel Weiss when their son, Ehrich, was born on March 24, 1874. The Weiss family was living in Budapest, the capital city of Hungary. Mr. Weiss was a rabbi, who led a small Jewish congregation.

The Weisses were poor. It was difficult to raise a family on a rabbi's small income. With four children to feed and dress, life was hard.

12

The same year Ehrich was born, Rabbi Weiss received a letter from America. In it was a job offer. The letter was from a group of Hungarians who had moved to America. They had settled in the small town of Appleton, Wisconsin. But there was no synagogue in Appleton. That meant there was no place for Jews to meet and pray together. Also, there was no rabbi to lead a congregation.

Samuel Weiss was asked to be the Appleton rabbi, at a salary of $750 a year. Even in 1874, $750 was not a big salary. But it was enough to make the Weisses want to leave Eastern Europe for the land of great promise.

The change wasn't difficult for the Weiss children. Herman, Nathan, William, and Ehrich were very young and learned English easily. It was not so easy for Mr. and Mrs. Weiss. They could speak, read, and write Hungarian and German, but learning English was a problem. After a while they stopped trying to learn the language of their new country.

Like many immigrant children, the Weiss brothers wanted to be American. But they also loved and respected their parents, who had never lost their European ways. This meant the children had to lead two lives. At home, the boys spoke German. Outside, they spoke English. At home, they behaved like old-fashioned, serious European children. Outside, they did everything their American-born friends did.

16

The new American ways were strange and frightening to Mr. and Mrs. Weiss. They worried that the children would get into trouble. But they had nothing to worry about. All their sons were well behaved, especially Ehrich. As Mrs. Weiss said, "Ehrich was a mother's dream. Never once did he cry when he was little. And when he did fuss, all I had to do was pick him up and hold him close."

She also said that when he was a baby, Ehrich never seemed to sleep. Any time she looked into his cradle, he was awake, watching every move she made. He was such a serious little boy, such a bright little boy. Surely, the Weisses agreed, Ehrich would be a scholar and a rabbi, just like his father.

Ehrich was indeed very bright. But he was not interested in religious studies. However, he could not tell his parents the truth. He loved them too much to hurt them that way, especially his mother. For as long as she lived, Ehrich adored his mother.

Since coming to America, the Weiss family had grown larger. There were three more children—Theo, Leopold, and Gladys. Now there were nine Weisses to feed and dress. Rabbi Weiss's salary was barely enough for all of them to live on.

Life was very difficult, but Mrs. Weiss didn't complain. Her happiness was her children. She took pleasure in cooking for them and in fixing the clothing of the older children to fit the younger

ones. Nothing seemed to bother her. For her children, Cecilia Weiss was a shield against the hardships of daily life.

The Weiss children knew the family needed money. So they all tried to help. From the age of eight, Ehrich worked after school. He sold newspapers and shined shoes. He brought home every penny he earned and gave it to his parents.

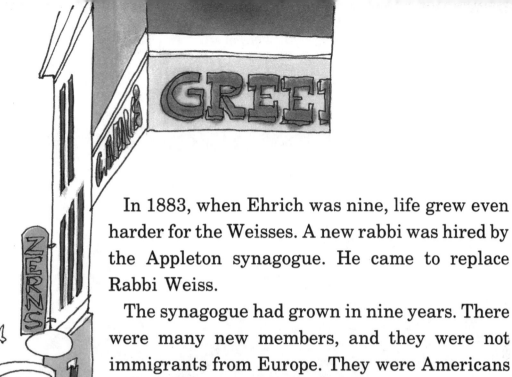

In 1883, when Ehrich was nine, life grew even harder for the Weisses. A new rabbi was hired by the Appleton synagogue. He came to replace Rabbi Weiss.

The synagogue had grown in nine years. There were many new members, and they were not immigrants from Europe. They were Americans who spoke English, and they wanted a rabbi who spoke their language. They respected Rabbi Weiss's learning, but that was not enough anymore.

Ehrich's father hoped to find work in the large city of Milwaukee. So he moved his family there. But things were no better in Milwaukee. No synagogue wanted to hire a rabbi who could not speak English. Rabbi Weiss earned a little money as a religious teacher. But it was not enough to support his large family. All the children old enough to work found ways to earn money for the family's needs.

Even so, Ehrich found time for fun. When a circus came to town, he went to see it with his younger brother, Theo. The boys saw things they had never seen before. There were clowns, elephants and tigers, sword swallowers, fire eaters, and a brass band. It was wonderful and exciting! Best of all, Ehrich told his mother, were the acrobats and the magician.

"The magician, Mama," Ehrich said, "you should have seen him! He can take rabbits and birds from an empty hat! He makes a red handkerchief turn into a blue one, then yellow—"

"But that's nothing!" Theo cut in. "He chops up a man—"

"Oh, that's terrible!" Mrs. Weiss said. "That's murder!" She covered her mouth with her hands, pretending to be shocked.

"Now, Mama," Ehrich said, "it isn't murder. It's magic. The magician cut off the man's arms and legs, and even his head. Of course, it wasn't too scary. The man was behind a curtain. So we couldn't see a lot of blood or anything.

"Anyway, when the magician finished, he threw the arms and legs and head behind the curtain. Then the drummer played *rat-a-tat-a-tat*. The magician opened the curtain—and the man was whole again."

24

"Oh, that's just a trick," Mrs. Weiss said.

"I know that," Ehrich told her. "But it's a magic trick. I wish I could do something like that. Everybody there just sat so still, watching. They didn't move. They didn't make a sound. Oh, if only I had that power!"

Ehrich promised himself that he would join the circus one day. First, he had to learn some skills. He did not know how to become a magician. But he could teach himself to do some acrobatics. And he found he was good at getting out of ropes tied around his wrists.

Ehrich and Theo practiced a rope-escape act every chance they got. Theo also learned a coin trick. He learned it from a photographer. For twenty-five cents a week, Theo ran errands for the photographer. But before paying Theo the quarter, the photographer always made it appear and disappear in his hand. Theo loved to watch the trick. One day he said, "Please teach me how to do that."

The photographer was glad to show Theo how the trick was done. Then Theo ran home to show Ehrich his new skill. Ehrich learned the trick quickly, using his left hand one time and then his right hand another.

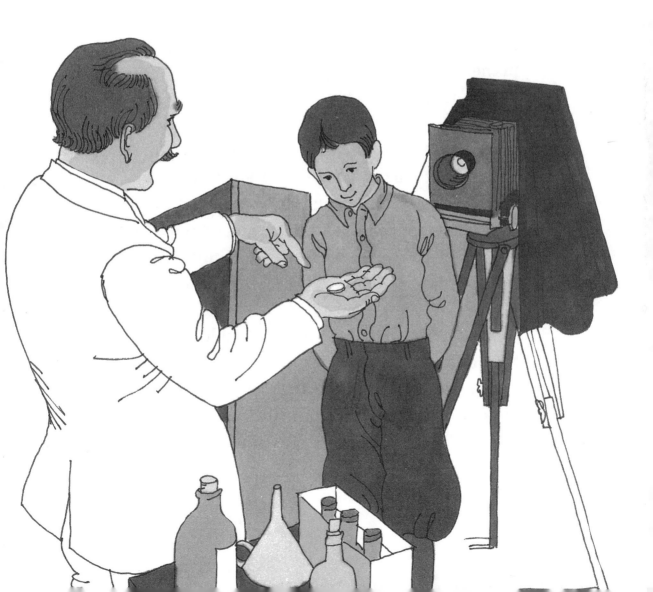

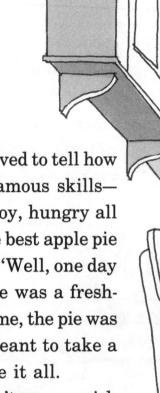

Years later, the Great Houdini loved to tell how he mastered yet another of his famous skills—opening locks. "I was a growing boy, hungry all the time. And my mother made the best apple pie in the world," Houdini explained. "Well, one day I came into the kitchen, and there was a fresh-baked pie cooling. Mama wasn't home, the pie was there, and I was hungry. I only meant to take a slice, but it was so good that I ate it all.

"Mama forgave that, and she didn't even punish me when it happened again. She just went out and bought a lock. When she finished baking, she put the pie into a kitchen cabinet and locked it.

"Well," Houdini continued, "there was only one thing to do. I had to learn how to open locks. When Mama found half a pie in a locked cabinet, she didn't know whether to laugh or spank me. All she did say was, 'I guess the cabinet opened itself. Right, Ehrie?'

"I told her that it was magic, and I had done it. Mama said that it was wonderful magic, but that I should do it on other locks—and leave her pies alone. So, being a good son, I opened locks all over. The only one I never touched again was in Mama's kitchen."

In 1887, the Weiss family moved to New York City. They hoped Rabbi Weiss would be able to open a religious school there. But he was no more successful in New York than he had been in Milwaukee. Fortunately, the Weiss children did get work. Ehrich, who was now thirteen, was a delivery boy for a department store.

In those days, there were no laws against young children working. For their work children were paid very little, much less than adults. So factories, stores, farms, and mines were always ready to hire children—some as young as four or five. Not until the twentieth century were laws passed to protect children from such abuse.

Department stores paid their delivery boys a very low salary. The delivery boys made their money from tips. The tips came from customers who received the packages. The more packages a boy delivered, the more money he earned. Ehrich and the other delivery boys moved as fast as they could through the streets of New York. In a good week, Ehrich might earn four dollars. But his usual earnings were about two dollars.

Even with the children working, the Weiss family just managed to survive. Some weeks they lived on a diet of soup, potatoes, and bread. They were always late paying their rent. And like many other poor people, they were terrified of being put out of their home by the landlord. This had happened to the Weisses five times during the four years they lived in Milwaukee. Ehrich had nightmares about this happening to them again.

In December 1887, it looked as if his nightmare might come true. The family had been in New York less than a year. Yet they already owed three months' rent. Then Ehrich had an idea. He printed these words on a card:

Christmas is coming.
Turkeys are fat.
Please drop a quarter
In the messenger boy's hat.

He pinned the card to his cap and wore it while delivering packages. People smiled when they read his poem. They also gave him much larger tips than usual. By the end of the week Ehrich

had collected a good deal of money. Before he got home on the last workday, he hid the coins all over himself—up his sleeves, under his collar, and in his hair.

Ehrich opened the apartment door and walked up to his mother. "Mama," he said, "shake me. I'm magic."

Mrs. Weiss took one of Ehrich's hands and shook it. Coins began to drop from his sleeve. She grabbed his shoulders and shook some more. This time coins tumbled from everywhere. The more she shook him, the more coins fell to the floor around Ehrich's feet. Mrs. Weiss was laughing and crying at the same time. "Oh, Ehrie, Ehrie," she said with delight, "now we can pay the rent."

After the Christmas season ended, the department store fired most of the boys. Ehrich was one of them. During the next few months, he worked as a messenger, a sweeper in a stable, and a photographer's helper. And he spent his spare time practicing magic tricks with his hands, called sleight of hand.

At the same time, he began to read everything he could find written about magic. All the books about magic said the same thing. The key to success was confidence. Confident people could do anything they set their minds to. Ehrich really believed those words.

In November 1888, Ehrich was out of work again. But he still had enough confidence in himself to find another job. This time, Ehrich became a cutter in a necktie factory, and he worked there for the next two and a half years.

His real interests, however, were in other things. As a member of the Pastime Athletic Club track team, he became a fine runner. He won many medals and ribbons. He also learned to swim and dive, and he competed successfully in those sports.

During this same time, Ehrich began to do daily exercise workouts in order to stay in shape. He continued to work out for the rest of his life. This was very important to him. The amazing escapes he did as the Great Houdini were possible only because of his remarkable strength and fitness.

The teenage Ehrich also wanted to feel confident in front of a large audience. So he joined a dramatic society. There, he learned how to behave on a stage and to speak clearly so that everyone could hear him. There were no microphones in those days. This meant performers had to have strong, trained voices.

Ehrich's athletic and dramatic hobbies were important, but they were not his main interest. The teen's real passion was magic. He studied how-to books of magic, attended magic shows, and visited stores that sold magic tricks and equipment.

One day, Ehrich came across a used copy of *Memoirs of Robert-Houdin.* Jean-Eugene Robert-Houdin was a nineteenth-century French magician. He had become famous and rich through his mastery of magic. Ehrich read the famous magician's book over and over. "From the moment I began to study the art of magic," Houdini said, "he became my guide and hero. I asked nothing more of life than to become in my profession like Robert-Houdin."

To show his admiration for his hero, the teen-age magician took the name "Houdini." His first name, "Harry," was what his friends called him. They did so because Mrs. Weiss's nickname for her son was "Ehrie," which sounded very much like "Harry."

Although he read about Robert-Houdin's magic tricks, Houdini himself never told anyone how he did his. That's why nobody knows exactly how he did his lock-opening tricks. We do know that Houdini worked very hard at sharpening his skills. He knew that every trick he performed had to look easy.

We also know that Houdini was fascinated by locks. Whenever he could, he visited locksmiths and manufacturers of bank safes. Houdini left nothing to chance. He never performed a trick or an escape until he was sure he would succeed. Learning all about locks was part of his preparation.

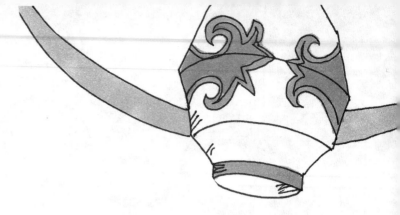

In 1891, the career of Harry Houdini was officially launched. The "Brothers Houdini," a magic team of Harry and his brother Theo, went on stage. They did card tricks; sleight of hand with handkerchiefs, flowers, and coins; and simple escape tricks. They were not very successful. The only work they could get was in dime museums.

A dime museum was like the sideshow of a circus. There were sword swallowers, fire eaters, and other attractions. It was the bottom of the show-business world. But Harry learned a lot. The sword swallowers taught him how to control his throat muscles. Contortionists, sometimes called human pretzels, taught him body control. These skills became important later in Harry's career.

What's more, young Harry Houdini was becoming a showman. He kept learning new tricks and better ways to present them. He grew steadily more confident in front of all kinds of audiences.

In 1894, while working in an amusement park in Brooklyn, Harry met a young singer named Bess Rahner. They fell in love and were married. It was a happy marriage. And Theo realized that Harry wanted to work with his new wife now. So the "Brothers Houdini" parted, with Theo going off on his own and Bess replacing him as Harry's magic partner. Bess was not a magician, but she quickly learned her part in the act and added much to their performance.

Harry Houdini did not become well known overnight. But every year brought him more fame. The big breakthrough came in 1900 when the Houdinis went to England. The British police had just developed a new kind of "escape-proof" handcuffs. Harry announced in public that he could escape from any handcuffs. The super-intendent of the British police accepted the challenge.

Houdini was told to put his arms around a large stone column. Then the handcuffs were snapped onto his wrists. The police superintendent told

Houdini that he would come back in an hour to unlock the cuffs.

All the police officials and newspaper reporters turned to leave. But before they reached the door, Houdini called out, "Wait! Don't you want your handcuffs?" He stood next to the column, smiling and holding up the opened cuffs.

Handcuffs played a smaller part in another, more dazzling escape made by Houdini. It *started* with him being handcuffed. Then Houdini was bound with ropes and chains. After that, he was locked inside a wooden crate. The trunk—weighted with six hundred pounds of iron—was dropped into New York City's East River. It sank instantly. But two minutes and fifty-five seconds later, Houdini popped to the surface—free of handcuffs, ropes, and chains. The escape took a magician's skills. It also demanded the body, training, and courage of a top athlete.

The news of Houdini's amazing escapes marked the beginning of a legend. In the years to come, he escaped from prison cells, bank vaults, armored trucks, straitjackets, and sealed coffins. He accepted every challenge. And with each success, his legend grew.

Houdini developed more and more difficult escapes. One of the most spectacular was his "Chinese Water Torture Cell." A large, clear-glass tank was placed on stage. It was filled with water. Houdini was then lowered upside down into the tank. His feet were chained to metal bars criss-crossing the tank's top. Then a curtain was drawn around the tank. Within minutes the master of magic appeared. His stunned audience could hardly believe what he had done.

Houdini invented and performed other amazing magic acts. These included walking through a brick wall and making an elephant vanish from the stage. After a while many people thought Houdini did truly supernatural things. But the Great Houdini always said, "All of my escapes are based on tricks. There is nothing mystical in what I do."

Year after year, his fame grew. He became what he set out to be: one of the world's greatest magicians. Until his death on Halloween night, October 31, 1926, Harry Houdini continued to amaze audiences everywhere. And even now, many years later, his name is still magic!